Drawn In

A PERFECTLY MESSY WAY TO EXPERIENCE JESUS

- writing well but scared to speak in front of others
- teaching my sister + brother
  frustrated when student couldn't learn quickly

Naturally liked / young disposition
building stuff, playing Barbies,
drawing + coloring, singing, playing
a tune on piano (one note by ear)
running fast, playing w/ brother,
taking care of sister + cousins,
cleaning + organizing, memorizing fast,
not comprehending well (both auditory +
some written instructions), puzzling

Very competitive — class president +
vice president 3 + 4 grade
when I liked my teachers
1st   2nd
Mrs ~~Myers~~ Mrs ~~Linden~~ Mrs Becker, Mrs Fee,
Mrs ~~Myers~~ Square dancing

5th + 6th grade — things fell apart @ home
7th grade ⊕⊕ math, science, track, bball
bullied   Valentines dance + ngr
~~track~~, camp, fire, fire
HS = fierce competition + band, angry + grouchy

Getting to know me again —
When mom was more capable
& Dad wasn't so out of control

I recall at an early age

    I enjoyed order & symmetry &

- Organization → arranging books from
  tall to short
  → making up sister's crib
  → reading hints from Helen

    I had an unusual talent for

THIS PAGE LEFT INTENTIONALLY BLANK.
(UNLESS YOU PUT SOMETHING ON IT.)
(WHICH YOU COULD, YOU KNOW.)
(AND THAT WOULD BE SO COOL.)
(HONEST. C'MON, GIVE IT A TRY.)

- putting things Together [mechanical]
  → bicycles → sewing Barbie
  clothes ⌐ pattern
  → not needing instruction manuals
  → knowing how to use tools
- running fast or enjoying speed
  when I zipped out
- having great hair
- doing art though I recall not
  being as talented as my friend
- shy around grown ups   →

Drawn In

A PERFECTLY MESSY WAY TO EXPERIENCE JESUS

Scripture quotations marked ASV are from the American Standard Version of the Bible, which is in the public domain.

Scripture quotations marked BSB are from the Berean Study Bible and are used with permission.

Scripture quotations marked CEB are taken from the Common English Bible®, CEB®. Copyright © 2010, 2011 by Common English Bible™. Used by permission. All rights reserved worldwide.

Scripture quotations marked CEV are from the Contemporary English Version. Copyright © 1991, 1992, 1995 by American Bible Society. Used by Permission.

Scripture quotations marked DLNT are from the Disciples' Literal New Testament. Copyright © 2011 Michael J. Magill. Used by permission. All rights reserved.

Scripture quotations marked ESV are from the ESV® Bible (The Holy Bible, English Standard Version®), copyright © 2001 by Crossway, a publishing ministry of Good News Publishers. Used by permission. All rights reserved.

God's Word is a copyrighted work of God's Word to the Nations. Quotations are used by permission. Copyright 1995 by God's Word to the Nations. All rights reserved.

Scripture quotations marked ISV are from the Holy Bible: International Standard Version®. Copyright © 1996-forever by The ISV Foundation. ALL RIGHTS RESERVED INTERNATIONALLY. Used by permission.

Scripture quotations marked NASB are taken from the New American Standard Bible®. Copyright © 1960, 1962, 1963, 1968, 1971, 1972, 1973, 1975, 1977, 1995 by The Lockman Foundation. Used by permission. (www.Lockman.org)

Scripture quotations designated (NET) are from the NET Bible® copyright © 1996-2006 by Biblical Studies Press, L.L.C. http://netbible.com. All rights reserved.

Scripture quotations marked NHEB are from the New Heart English Bible and are used with permission.

Scripture quotations marked NIV are taken from THE HOLY BIBLE, NEW INTERNATIONAL VERSION®, NIV®. Copyright © 1973, 1978, 1984, 2011 by Biblica, Inc.® Used by permission. All rights reserved worldwide.

Scripture quotations marked NLT are taken from the Holy Bible, New Living Translation, copyright © 1996, 2004, 2015 by Tyndale House Foundation. Used by permission of Tyndale House Publishers, Inc., Carol Stream, Illinois 60188. All rights reserved.

Scripture quotations marked WNT are from the Weymouth New Testament and are used with permission.

ISBN 978-1-4707-4285-0

10 9 8 7 6 5 4 3 2 1   25 24 23 22 21 20 19 18 17 16

Printed in China.

Hungry for a Jesus-Centered Life?

It's great to learn about Jesus—to study, soak in sermons, and highlight Bible verses.

But to *know* Jesus? Live a life orbiting tightly around him?

That takes more. It takes relationship. And peeling back the answers to two important questions:

1. Who do you say *Jesus* is?
2. And who does Jesus say *you* are?

Grappling with those two questions draws you deeper into an authentic relationship with Jesus. One that's honest and transparent...and lets you see him—and yourself—clearly.

These 40 devotions carve out space for you to pause and catch your breath. To consider those two questions. To let Jesus speak to you about himself, about you, and about your friendship with him.

So come.

Come draw closer to Jesus—in a fresh way.

Come take your next steps into the joy and peace of a Jesus-centered life.

> # Come to me, all you who are
> # **weary and burdened,**
> ## and I will give you rest.

—Jesus

(Matthew 11:28, NIV)

Realized from an early age I thought differently than most of my family, except maybe my Dad. We seemed to engage life similarly + were more impulsive.

In HS I realized I was more mature than both my parents + started to try to control things.

Imagine a life in which you're no longer doing all the stuff you should be doing for Jesus and instead you're just...*with* Jesus.

Consider how that might feel as you color in this sign—any shade you like.

Stop wasting energy pretending I am less than I am

Pray | Jesus, help me get past the busywork of my "shoulds" so that I'm simply resting in you.

Drawn In

Here it is again
    another year past.

All is improved but the same
    things remain off track
        – my focus + ability to complete
            tasks
        – my weight 2° unhealthy
                eating + sedentary lifestyle
        – my sense of self-discipline
        + now that when it comes
        to many things, it doesn't
        really matter anyway

Once again, I want these
    to change in

        low self confidence
regarding pessimism personal
            HOPE, and an effective
    tools of the devil.

$$\boxed{186}$$

(Should) — crossed out

∞

I should be grown up.

I will grow with Jesus.

What does grown up look like?

This is a midlife crossroad.

Jesus

★

Service — Health — Wealth
family ★ Marriage

Confusion
ipracticality
too much time
inactivity
poor self discipline
downer attitude

> "But God demonstrates His own **love toward us,** in that while we were yet sinners, Christ died for us.
>
> (Romans 5:8, NASB)

God doesn't make mistakes. I am not a mistake. I matter. We all take things for granted until tragedy strikes. Be ever vigilant & grateful for the present.

I am enough...
BECAUSE
He is
ENOUGH

I am Here

✏️ Say it once...
then again. Out loud.

✏️ Repeat it, emphasizing first one word,
and then the next.

I am enough...

I **am** enough...

I am **enough**...

You get the idea.

a big heart heart enough to care for my whole family as a very young person to see what needed to be done so all felt safe + cared for

You're enough. Enough to be loved by Jesus. Rescued by Jesus. To draw close to Jesus.

That's how I — became a door — natural ability w/ the wrong fertilizer spread unhealthy comparison

---

Pray | Jesus, it's not always easy to feel as if I'm enough. To feel worthy. Help me see myself as you see me,

Drawn In

2016

2017

add icicle lights

down
around both sides of the house

need 5 more strands

more wreaths on windows

$$185$$
$$- 35$$
$$\overline{150}$$ size
8-10

$$\begin{array}{r} 2 \\ 35 \\ \times 1.5 \text{ wk} \\ \hline 175 \\ 35 \\ \hline 52.5 \end{array}$$

52 weeks/year

(2017)

sit ups   50
push ups   20
squats   #500 lay on thighs
touch toes

(150)

> The woman said, 'I know the **Messiah is coming**–the one who is called Christ. When he comes, he will explain everything to us.' Then Jesus told her, 'I am the Messiah!'

(John 4:25-26, NLT)

2020 Climbing into Papa Bear's lap just to be held + comforted through difficult emotional + physical times

It wants me to go for it.

"Lord, you have searched me, and you know me. You know my sitting down and my rising up. You perceive **my thoughts** from afar. You search out my path and my lying down, and are acquainted with all my ways."

(Psalm 139:1-3, NHEB)

What's one thing about Jesus you're unshakably sure is true? And one thing you're pretty sure is false?

✒ Jot them here:

True Perfect Love for Humanity + Reconciliation to Him

False _____

Pray | Jesus, how would you answer the same questions about me?

✒ Jot what Jesus tells you here:

True Heart

False Selfish

So self-protection was needed from my parents. Cast as selfishness by harsh judgment + non-compassion Mom

Drawn In

Self Involved parents ~~have~~ have little or no ability to reflect their childrens strengths.

If I don't know & easy identify my own strengths, I cannot do well to recognize those in my children — + hesban

Children become embarrassed to think of themselves in terms of their most positive qualities.

highly sensitive vs overly sensitive
→ big heart → vulnerable, easily influenced

My Strengths

- discernment
- intuition
- heart for children
- highly sensitive
- thoughtful — deep thinking

"When I was a child,
I **spoke** and **thought**
and **reasoned** as
a child. But when
I grew up, I put away
childish things."

(1 Corinthians 13:11, NLT)

Find—or remember—a childhood photo of yourself. Cute kid, huh?

When you were a child, what did you think and feel about Jesus?
In what ways have those thoughts and feelings shifted over the years?

✏️ Capture your thoughts here:

Think of yourself in terms of your most positive qualities.

It's crucial to know what your assets are ± be able to articulate them.

Provides SELF-VALIDATION + allows you to feel good about what you bring to this world?!

JESUS ☆ IS MY ☺ ☆ FRiEND

Pray | Jesus, what else are you ready for me to discover about you?

Drawn In

A PERFECTLY MESSY WAY TO EXPERIENCE JESUS

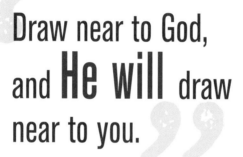

"Draw near to God, and **He will** draw near to you."

(James 4:8a, WNT)

Ask Jesus: What's standing between the two of us?

✏️ Listen, hear, and then graffiti the answer onto this wall using paint, pencil, lipstick—whatever's handy.

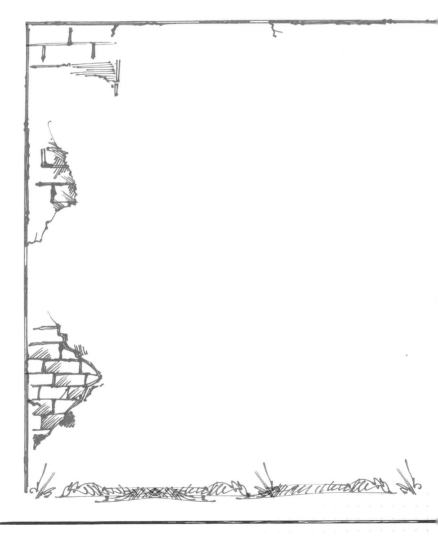

 Jesus, help me understand why I leave this wall standing... and what would happen if I tore it down.

Drawn In

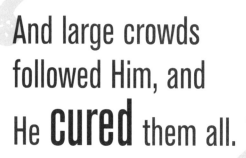

" And large crowds
followed Him, and
He **cured** them all. "

(Matthew 12:15b, DLNT)

- ✎ On the bandages list any broken bones, scars, surgeries, and other and boo-boos you've accumulated in life.

- ✎ Include your invisible hurts, too: ruptured relationships, sprained self-images, and emotional ouchies.

- ✎ Then head to the medicine cabinet, find real bandages, and cover up those on the page. That's what Jesus' love can do for you: bring healing to the broken places.

Pray | Jesus, are you still healing people? What needs healing in me?

Drawn In

> " And behold, I am **with you always,** to the end of the age. "

–Jesus

(Matthew 28:20b, ESV)

- ✏️ Ask Jesus: Where do I go that—so far—I don't invite you to come along?

- ✏️ As Jesus brings those places to mind, list them here...or not.

- ✏️ And then invite him...or not.

 Pray | Jesus, how would my life change if I invited you into all of it?

Drawn In

"Don't let your **hearts be troubled.** Believe in God, believe also in me. "

–Jesus

(John 14:1, ISV)

Believing and trusting:
easier said than done.

✏️ Ask Jesus where he'd say your trust in him falls in these three areas: your relationship with him, your bank account, and your most messed-up relationship with someone else.

✏️ Mark one thermometer for each.

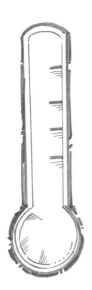  

Pray | Jesus, what do these marks say about me? About you? About our relationship?

Drawn In

A PERFECTLY MESSY WAY TO EXPERIENCE JESUS

"He is so rich in **kindness** and grace that he purchased our **freedom** with the blood of his Son and **forgave** our sins.

✏️ With a pencil, write or draw that thing that haunts you. That you can't get past. That you did, or left undone, that harmed yourself or others. Write or draw it...look at it...then erase it.

Because that's what Jesus did. He'll forgive you. Can you forgive yourself?

Pray | Jesus, help me offer myself the same grace you've lavished on me.

Drawn In

A PERFECTLY MESSY WAY TO EXPERIENCE JESUS (J.)

"I have much more to say to you, but right now it would be more than you could **understand.**"

–Jesus

(John 16:12, CEV)

✏️ Fill this question mark with question marks—
as many as you can stuff in there.

If you could ask Jesus any question, and get a clear answer, what would you ask—and why?

✏️ Jot it down—Jesus welcomes your questions.

Drawn In

"For the law of the Spirit of life in Christ Jesus has **set you free** from the law of sin and of death."

(Romans 8:2, NASB)

Free. You are free.

Free to embrace joy, soak in gratitude, grab hold of the life God's spread out before you.

So shout it. Dance it. Sing it out. *Free!*

 Lift this book to the heavens and close your eyes as you let his love flow through you. Free!

Pray | Jesus, you've set me free—now what's next?

Drawn In

A PERFECTLY MESSY WAY TO EXPERIENCE JESUS

'Well,' they replied, 'some say **John the Baptist,** some say **Elijah,** and others say you are one of the other **ancient prophets** risen from the dead.' Then he asked them, **'But who do you say I am?'**

(Luke 9:19-20, NLT)

Jesus asked his disciples who they said he was.

How do you answer Jesus' question?
Who is Jesus to you?

✏ Write it on the name tag.

Hello
my name is

Pray | Jesus, show me the real you.

Drawn In

A PERFECTLY MESSY WAY TO EXPERIENCE JESUS

"This means that he had to **become like his people** in every way, in order to be their faithful and merciful High Priest in his service to God, so that the people's sins would be forgiven."

(Hebrews 2:17, GNT)

✏️ On this page write the names of a half-dozen people you love. Or sketch their portraits.

✏️ Then ask Jesus how he's like everyone on your page... and how he's completely different.

Drawn In

"You are the **light of the world.** A city set on a hill cannot be hidden."

–Jesus

(Matthew 5:14, NASB)

Jesus made you to shine. How are you shining?

✏️ Write or draw where Jesus is telling you to shine today.

Drawn In

A PERFECTLY MESSY WAY TO EXPERIENCE JESUS **J.**

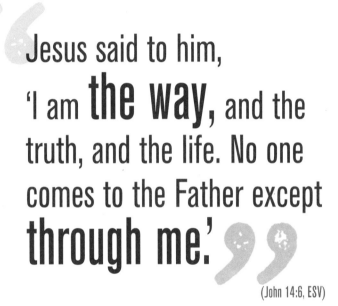

Jesus said to him, 'I am **the way,** and the truth, and the life. No one comes to the Father except **through me.'**

(John 14:6, ESV)

Pray | Jesus, your words still stop some people in their tracks. Your claim sounds so exclusive. Divisive. Arrogant, even.

But those are your words… and you didn't say them lightly.

What do they tell me about you? And what do I do with the parts of you that make me feel uncomfortable?

✏️ Color in these signs—any colors you want. As you do, listen for Jesus to answer your prayer.

Drawn In

A PERFECTLY MESSY WAY TO EXPERIENCE JESUS

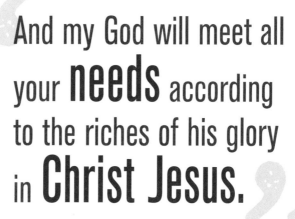

"And my God will meet all your **needs** according to the riches of his glory in **Christ Jesus.**"

(Philippians 4:19, NIV)

What does it take for you to be happy? Jesus, sure, but what else?

✏ Fill in the blanks.

Jesus + _____ = Happy

Jesus + _____ = Happy

Jesus + _____ = Happy

Jesus + _____ = Happy

Jesus + _____ = Happy

Jesus + _____ = Happy

✏ Now check your list. How much is temporary? Necessary? How much will bring you lasting joy and eternal life?

Pray | Jesus, if I have you...what else do I need? What will it take for me to see you as enough?

Drawn In

A PERFECTLY MESSY WAY TO EXPERIENCE JESUS **J.**

> " I love all who love me.
> Those who **search**
> will surely find me. "
>
> (Proverbs 8:17, NLT)

If your relationship with Jesus had a color, what color would it be? And why would it be that color?

✎ Pick a color. Put a blob of that color in the frame below—in pencil, pen, ketchup, paint—whatever. Then stick your thumb in the blob to leave your mark.

Pray | Jesus, what does that color say about my feelings toward you? And what color would you choose to reflect your feelings toward me?

Drawn In

"My sheep hear **my voice,** and I know them, and they **follow me.**"

—Jesus

(John 10:27, ASV)

Pray | What words do you have for me today, Jesus? I'm listening...

 Jot what you hear in the text bubble.

Drawn In

A PERFECTLY MESSY WAY TO EXPERIENCE JESUS

"Then Jesus said to Thomas, 'Put your finger here and look at My hands. Reach out your hand and put it into My side. **Stop doubting and believe.**"

(John 20:27, BSB)

Maybe you think of *doubt* as a four-letter word. That it signals a lack of faith... skepticism...spiritual failure.

"#!@*"
(doubt)

What does Jesus' response to Thomas tell you about how Jesus deals with doubt?

 Find a spot where you can be alone and tell Jesus your doubts—out loud. See what happens.

Pray | Jesus, do you love me—even with my doubts?

Drawn In

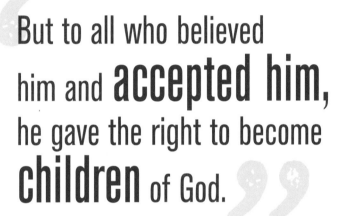

"But to all who believed him and **accepted him,** he gave the right to become **children** of God."

(John 1:12, NLT)

You've been invited...
adopted...accepted.

Jesus calls you his own—a cherished member of his family.

✏ Fill in the birth announcement.
Because with Jesus, you belong.

BECAUSE OF

Jesus,

_____

❈ God is pleased ❈
to announce

THE ARRIVAL OF

_____

Added to the family of God!

DATE: _____

 Pray | Jesus, you've called me your own. I love you for that. Walk with me as I find more and deeper ways to call you mine, too.

Drawn In

"I can do **everything** through Christ who **strengthens** me."

(Philippians 4:13, *God's Word*)

Life can be a challenge.

Finances. Friendships. Jobs. Kids. Parents. Life.

You don't have to chug up those hills under your own steam alone.

 What hills do you need Jesus' help in climbing?

Pray | Jesus, I need your help. If I'm in the way, show me how.

Drawn In

Color in the names that Jesus speaks to you and let them linger as you consider: Why those names? What might Jesus be saying to you about himself?

The Truth   Son of God
Alpha and Omega
Master   Morning Star
Righteous One   Savior
Great Physician   Son of God
Lion of Judah
King of the Jews   Faithful Witness
Bridegroom
Holy   Immanuel

Counselor Rabbi
The Rock
Living Water Lord
Shepherd
High Priest Man of
Sorrows
Mediator Bread of Life
Cornerstone
King Deliverer
Judge
Redeemer Lamb
Creator

Pray | Jesus, which of your names do you want me to embrace right now?

Drawn In

"After he took his seat at the table with them, he took the bread, blessed and broke it, and gave it to them. Their **eyes were opened** and they recognized him, but he disappeared from their sight."

(Luke 24:30-31, CEB)

✏️ Without looking at it, draw the front of your cell phone. Every button, screen, and scratch. Fill in as many details as possible. Then pull out the real thing and compare it with your sketch. How'd you do?

Hmm. Given how often you've looked at your phone, how did you miss so much?

Sometimes what's familiar fades into the background.

Drawn In

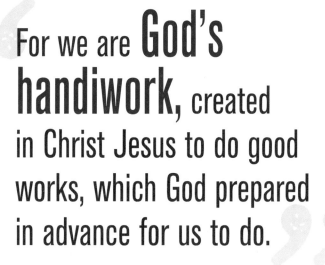

"For we are **God's handiwork,** created in Christ Jesus to do good works, which God prepared in advance for us to do."

(Ephesians 2:10, NIV)

You're unique. One of a kind.

And created to love Jesus and do good in his world. Good that you're perfectly designed to do.

 Dirty a finger with soot, dirt, or ink. Place your fingerprint here:

Pray | Jesus, what good works have you prepared me to do?

Drawn In

"So then, if anyone is in Christ, he is a **new creation;** what is old has passed away—look, what is new has come!

(2 Corinthians 5:17, NET)

✏️ Draw a portrait of yourself...as a baby. Stretched out on a rug, gazing adoringly at a teddy bear—capture your too-cute-to-be-believed, dimpled, most wonderful self.

That's you when you were fresh and new. And that's you now.

Pray | Jesus, help me see myself as you see me.

Drawn In

Jesus said to him, 'If you would be perfect, go, sell what you possess and give to the poor, and you will have **treasure in heaven;** and come, follow me.' When the young man heard this he went away sorrowful, for he had great possessions.

(Matthew 19:21-22, ESV)

Yes! Ano! A-yo!
Avunu! Gee! Hanji!
Si! Ja! Na'am! Oo! Ho! Da! Nai!
Oui! Taip! Hai! Huffi!
Ndiyo! Evet! Tak! Shi! Baleh!

✏ Draw symbols of ways you're saying yes to Jesus.

What's Jesus bringing into your life through those yeses?

Jesus, how are you inviting me to say yes to you today?

Drawn In

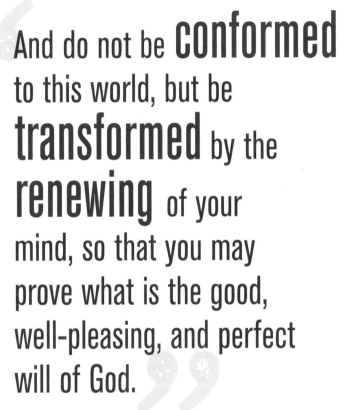

And do not be **conformed** to this world, but be **transformed** by the **renewing** of your mind, so that you may prove what is the good, well-pleasing, and perfect will of God.

(Romans 12:2, NHEB)

Holy. Faultless.

Because of Jesus, that's how God sees you.
He's looking through the lenses of grace and
perfect love.

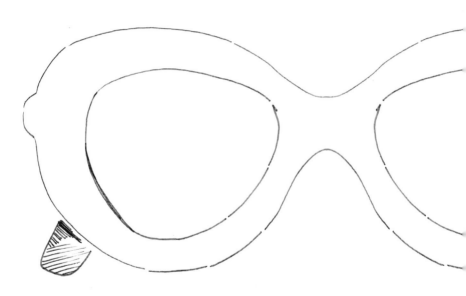 Transform these frames into designer
delights as you repeat the following to
yourself: Holy. Faultless. Beloved. Transformed.

 Jesus, help me see myself the way you see me.

Drawn In

A PERFECTLY MESSY WAY TO EXPERIENCE JESUS

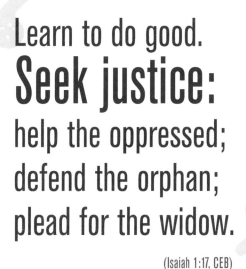

"Learn to do good.
Seek justice:
help the oppressed;
defend the orphan;
plead for the widow."

(Isaiah 1:17, CEB)

Jesus cared about lots of people.

Especially people living on the margins.

✏️ Ask him which social issue in the news he cares most about. Then consider caring about it yourself.

Drawn In

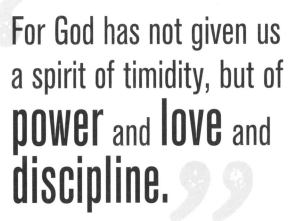

For God has not given us a spirit of timidity, but of **power** and **love** and **discipline.**

(2 Timothy 1:7, NASB)

✏️ Since Jesus is with you, what's something you'll risk doing this week?

R
I
S
K

Pray | Jesus, what will it take for me to trust you more fully? To live a life free of fear?

Drawn In

A PERFECTLY MESSY WAY TO EXPERIENCE JESUS

Then Jesus told his disciples, 'If anyone would come after me, let him **deny himself** and take up his cross and follow me.'

(Matthew 16:24, ESV)

Not all of Jesus' followers went the distance. Not once it started straining relationships. Demanding change. Requiring forgiveness.

They were in...but not all in.

✎ Ask Jesus: In what ways do you want me to be all in?

Drawn In

A PERFECTLY MESSY WAY TO EXPERIENCE JESUS

"But we are **citizens** of heaven, where the Lord Jesus Christ lives. And we are eagerly waiting for him **to return** as our Savior."

(Philippians 3:20, NLT)

You're a citizen of heaven.

It's the home you were made for.

In every sense of the word, with every ounce of your being—
heaven is where you belong. Forever.

 Since that's where you're headed, draw a "heaven"
stamp on this passport.

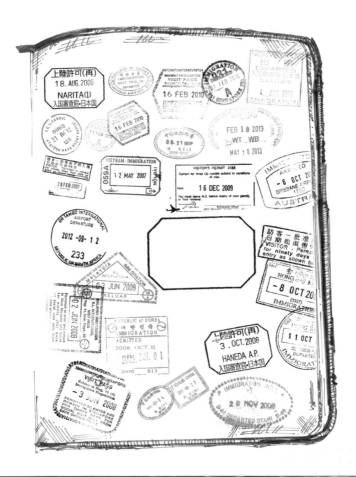

Pray | Jesus, thank you for the promise of heaven.
       | Help me sense heaven now.

Drawn In

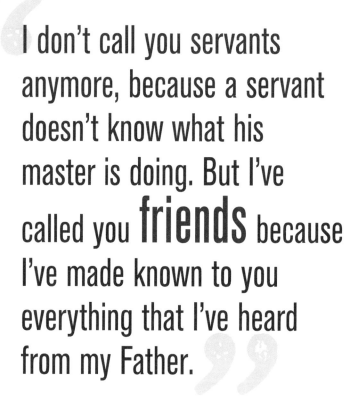

"I don't call you servants anymore, because a servant doesn't know what his master is doing. But I've called you **friends** because I've made known to you everything that I've heard from my Father."

–Jesus

(John 15:15, *God's Word*)

> # **Friend** (frend)
> {noun}
>
> 1. A person you know and with whom you have a bond of mutual affection or esteem.
>
> 2. Someone of the same group you're in.
>
> 3. A favored companion.

Friend.

That's what Jesus calls you...does it feel true?

✏️ In what ways is Jesus your friend?

 Jesus, help me draw close to you as the friend you are. Open my heart to your friendship, Jesus.

Drawn In

A PERFECTLY MESSY WAY TO EXPERIENCE JESUS

He said to them, 'You are the ones who **justify yourselves** in the eyes of others, but God knows **your hearts.**'

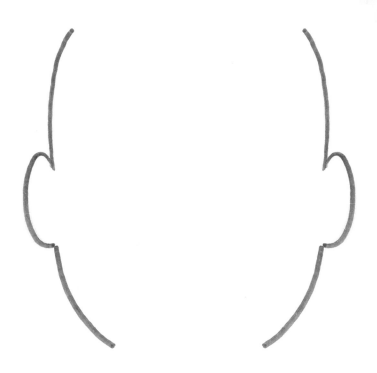 Draw a mask—the one you wear to keep everyone happy at work, at home, at church. Sketch the "you" that you show the world.

How well does it fool you? How well do you think it fools Jesus?

 When you've finished, pull out your phone and take a selfie. Look at the photo as you pray.

Pray | Jesus, who am I when all my masks are torn away? Who do you say I am?

Drawn In

A PERFECTLY MESSY WAY TO EXPERIENCE JESUS J.

"And you are not your own, for you have been **redeemed** at **infinite cost.**"

(1 Corinthians 6:20a, WNT)

You're worth it to Jesus.

Worth sleeping on rocky, Palestinian ground. Worth coping with hunger and the snipes of petty religious leaders. Worth being fawned over, ignored, and betrayed. Worth crucifixion.

✏ Trace your hand.

✏ Draw a nail hole on the hand you've traced.

That's what you're worth to him.

 *Pray* | Jesus, thank you.

Drawn In

A PERFECTLY MESSY WAY TO EXPERIENCE JESUS J.

"Are not five sparrows sold for two pennies? Yet not one of them is forgotten by God. Indeed, the very **hairs** of **your of head** are all numbered. Don't be afraid; you are worth more than many sparrows."

–Jesus

(Luke 12:6-7, NIV)

Jesus knows you. *Really* knows you, intimately.
No other relationship even comes close.

How does that feel?

 Tape one of your hairs here.

Drawn In

"In the beginning, the Word existed. The Word was with God, and the Word was God. He existed in the beginning with God. Through him **all things were made,** and apart from him nothing was made that has been made."

(John 1:1-3, ISV)

✏️ Before pressing a piece of nature between these pages, look closely at it. What does this tidbit of his creation tell you about Jesus?

Press a blade of grass,
flower, or leaf between
the pages here.

 Jesus, help me see you in your handiwork—myself included.

Drawn In

A PERFECTLY MESSY WAY TO EXPERIENCE JESUS **J.**

"I am the vine; you are the branches. The one who **remains in me**–and I in him–bears much fruit, because **apart from me** you can accomplish nothing."

—Jesus

(John 15:5, NET)

Staying connected to Jesus—it's a good idea.

Your friendship deepens...you live more vibrantly...you produce more fruit. There's life and joy and hope.

 How closely connected are you?
Write or draw your answer.

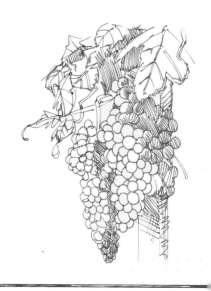

Pray | Jesus, what am I doing on my own that would be far easier—and more impactful—if I let you power it in my life?

Drawn In

But he said to me, 'My grace is **sufficient for you,** for my power is made **perfect in weakness.'** Therefore I will boast all the more gladly of my weaknesses, so that the power of Christ may rest upon me.

(2 Corinthians 12:9, ESV)

✏️ See if you can balance this book perfectly level on one fingertip.

Not quite that coordinated? No problem—because your perfection isn't the point. It never has been.

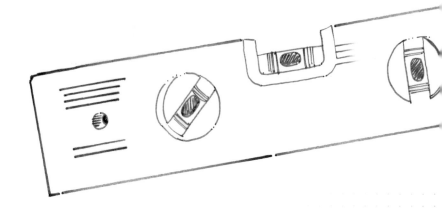

Drawn In

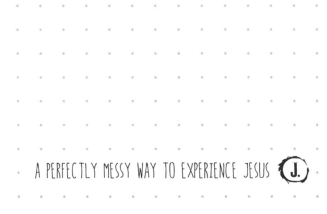

A PERFECTLY MESSY WAY TO EXPERIENCE JESUS

"And he will be called:

Wonderful Counselor, Mighty God, Everlasting Father, Prince of Peace. "

(Isaiah 9:6b, NLT)

These words from Isaiah describe Jesus, the One seeking to know you more fully. The One whose love reaches out to you.

✏️ Find a place to be alone and read these descriptions of Jesus aloud. Again…and again. Let them wash through you, feed your spirit, nurture your soul.

✏️ As words call out to you, circle them. Then thank Jesus for the ways he's shown himself to you. Write or draw them here.

 Pray | Jesus, fill me. Give me eyes to see you as you are, and a heart that swells with wonder at you.

Drawn In

A PERFECTLY MESSY WAY TO EXPERIENCE JESUS

Drawn In

Drawn In

Drawn In